Little Business Books

Change

Written by **Ruth Percival**

Illustrated by **Dean Gray**

W

FRANKLIN WATTS

LONDON · SYDNEY

First published in Great Britain in 2024
by Hodder & Stoughton

Credits
Series Editor: Amy Pimperton
Series Designer: Peter Scoulding
Consultant: Philippa Anderson
Philippa Anderson has a business degree and is a writer
and communications consultant who advises multinationals.
She authors and contributes to business books.

HB ISBN: 978 1 4451 8569 9
PB ISBN: 978 1 4451 8570 5

Printed in Dubai

Franklin Watts
An imprint of
Hachette Children's Group
Part of Hodder & Stoughton
Carmelite House
50 Victoria Embankment
London EC4Y 0DZ

An Hachette UK Company

www.hachette.co.uk
www.hachettechildrens.co.uk

Contents

What is change?

Change is when something becomes different.

Winter changes into spring. Your body changes as you grow older. Baking changes ingredients into a cake.

Sometimes change is something you can feel. You might change your mind about something. Change can sometimes make you feel worried if you don't know what will happen next.

WHY IS CHANGE IMPORTANT?

In business, change is important. Change might mean inventing a new product, serving new customers or moving to a bigger place.

For you, change might mean moving house or being brave enough to try something new.

What will our animal friends find out about change in business and about themselves?

Get ready for change

Everyone plays outside on warm, sunny days.
Customers buy lots of bikes, kites and footballs
from Enzo Elephant's toy shop.

Storms are coming!

Enzo predicts a change.
He phones the toy warehouse.

The next day, indoor toys and games arrive – along with storm clouds!

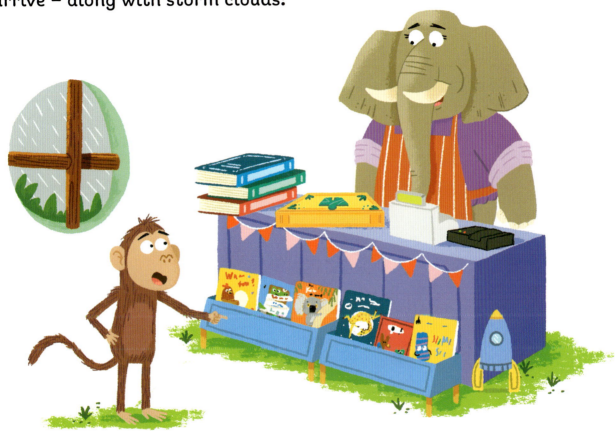

Enzo Elephant's customers are delighted. Now they have toys to play with inside while it rains outside!

Knowing change is coming helps you to be ready.

Try new things

Pip Penguin's ice tours are AMAZING, but very expensive. Something needs to change to attract more customers.

Pip Penguin has a brilliant idea – virtual reality ice tours!
They will be less expensive, but just as much fun!

Change can encourage you to try new things.

Challenge accepted!

Customers love Peggy Polar Bear's fun snow animal statues. But Wei Wolf wants Peggy to make him a snow garden instead!

Changing her product will be a challenge, but Peggy accepts!

Peggy Polar Bear gets creative ... and makes Wei Wolf an amazing snow and ice garden.

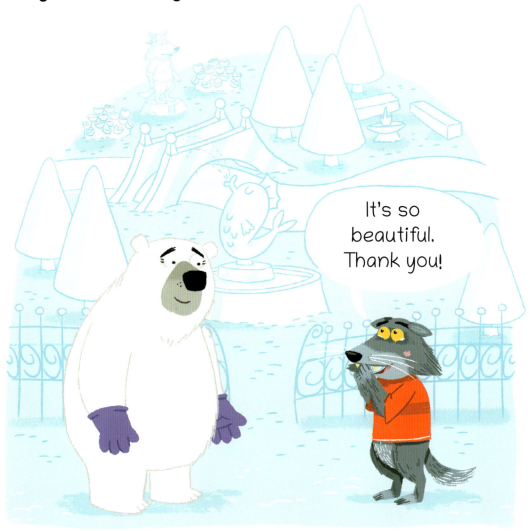

Try to stay positive when change brings challenges.

A better idea

Even when wearing her best trainer design,
Tilly Tiger can't beat Chip Cheetah in a race.

You can't catch me!

Tilly decides to change her trainer design to help her go faster.

Tilly Tiger spends ages drawing.
She does lots of research, too.

It's race day!

GO!

Tilly wins!

My new trainers
are super-fast!

Remember, some changes take time and effort to make.

A new idea

Wei Wolf wonders why birds don't buy his caps.

It's because they blow off when we fly fast.

Wei invents a new product just for birds. Hats with chinstraps!

Omar Owl and his friends buy lots of the new hats.

These hats are perfect for birds!

Thinking about what others need helps you to change your ideas.

Learn from others

Customers are queuing to get a table at Peter Panda's pizza restaurant. But he can't serve everyone – there isn't enough space.

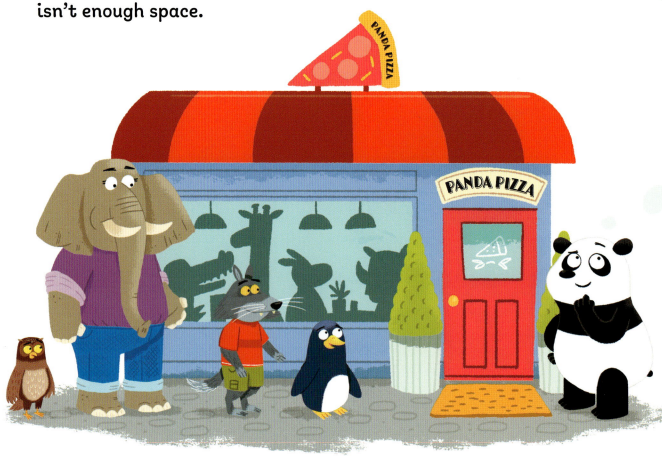

Peter sees Kit Kangaroo zipping past delivering cakes. This gives Peter a great idea.

Peter Panda opens a new pizza delivery service.
Now everyone can enjoy his delicious pizzas!

Learning from others can inspire you to change.

Swap over

Kit Kangaroo's café has a problem. Pip Penguin keeps burning the cakes and Tilly Tiger has mixed up the orders – again!

I have an idea. Let's swap over your jobs.

It turns out that Tilly Tiger is an expert baker. And Pip Penguin remembers everything!

Now the café runs perfectly.

Be open to swapping things around.

Work together

There's chaos at Kiki Koala's tree farm! Everyone is making mistakes because they aren't working as a team.

Kiki knows what needs to change.

You all need to work together.

Now, instead of everyone doing jobs by themselves, they help one another with each task in turn. This simple change helps the whole team to work better together.

Change feels good when you work with others.

21

Be flexible

Chip Cheetah hires Omar Owl as a yoga instructor.

But Omar keeps falling asleep in class!

I like to sleep in the day!

To solve the problem, Chip Cheetah lets Omar Owl work at night.

Customers love the new night classes and Omar is happier, too.

Being flexible means you can adapt to change.

A change for the better

Milly Monkey wonders why her customers are grumpy when they leave her zip wire adventure park. Haven't they had fun?

Milly Monkey makes a smart change. The last zip wire now ends near the exit. This change makes her business more organised – and more fun.

Change can make a good thing even better.

Change old for new

Omar Owl's kite-making machine is very old.

It keeps going wrong.

The machine has tangled up the string!

What a mess! Omar knows he must buy a new machine, or his business won't have anything to sell.

The new kite-making machine is AMAZING!

Omar Owl is pleased he made a change!

When things go wrong, a change could fix the problem.

A bigger place

Roarsome Cars has a big problem. Leon Lion
has too many cars in his tiny garage and
it's putting off customers.

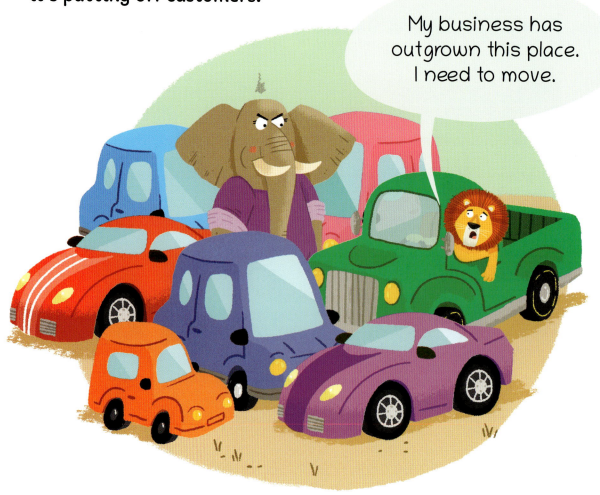

Leon Lion finds the perfect new garage,
with lots of space for his cars!

When you outgrow things, it is a good time to make a change.

Change and you

Our animal friends have learned a lot about change in business. What they have learned can help you, too!

Tilly Tiger made her product even better.
Change can help you to keep improving and learning.

Enzo Elephant was organised and prepared.
Change is often easier to deal with when you know it is coming.

Chip Cheetah was flexible.
When you can adapt to change, you can solve problems quickly and your confidence and resilience get stronger.

Notes for sharing this book

This book introduces business ideas around the topic of change, which link to core personal and social skills, such as teamwork, listening and being fair.

Talk to the child or class about what business is and why we need good businesses. You can use each scenario to discuss change themes. For example, talk about a time when the child was inspired by others to make a positive change.

Change can sometimes feel scary, but it is important to be open to new ideas and experiences and have faith in our ability to cope with change. Talk about a time when the child experienced a change, such as starting a new school. How did they feel before and after?

Glossary

adapt to change something to use it in a new way

business a company that buys, makes or sells goods or services to make money

chaos a mess; confusion

customer someone who buys things from a business

effort to try very hard

expert someone who is very skilled at something; someone who knows a lot about a topic

flexible able to adapt easily to changing circumstances

hire to take on someone to work for you

inspire to make someone feel like they want to do something

invent to create or design something new

predict to say or think that something will happen in the future

products the goods or services that a business makes or sells

research to look carefully into something to see what more you can learn

virtual reality a world made by a computer program that feels and sounds real to the person using it

warehouse a big building where goods are stored before they are sold